The SVN Difference

Creating a Culture of Trust in Commercial Real Estate

By
Diane K. Danielson

With
Kevin Maggiacomo,
George Slusser and Solomon Poretsky

The SVN Difference: Creating a Culture of Trust in Commercial Real Estate

Cover Design: 3Thought Creative

Marketing Department
SVN International Corp.
33 Arch Street, Floor 17
Boston, MA 02110
or email your request to marketing@svn.com.

ISBN-13 (print): 978-0692069882
ISBN-10 (print): 0692069887

Printed in the United States of America

Dedication

This book is dedicated to our SVN® franchise owners, Advisors and staff. Without you, we would not be SVN!

Your enthusiasm and dedication to the brand has helped create a unique and amazing culture of trust.

Table of Contents

Preface

I started my career at SVN International Corp. (SVNIC) in 2001 in a sales role. As the company expanded, so did my knowledge of the business. I took this knowledge and grew my role serving as vice president of our franchise business and chief operating officer before being appointed president in 2008. In the nearly two decades since I joined, the SVN® brand has grown and evolved, yet continues to embrace the fundamental principles on which the company was founded. This is an astounding accomplishment in a sometimes-tumultuous industry that is often stuck in an era of days gone by.

While other companies wavered as the country clawed its way back from the economic downturn, SVNIC set forth on a strategic growth plan for the brand. First, we polished up our core covenants while keeping the original messaging, and then did the same with our mission statement:

To create amazing value with our clients, colleagues, and communities.

Based on that mission, and under the guidance of our founder, Mark Van Ness, and the rest of our leadership team, we are collectively embracing and expanding upon a business growth strategy that runs counter to that of our competitors. When we list properties, we share fees. Essentially, we crowdsource for the best buyers. We publicize listings to the market with an incentive fee for anyone bringing a buyer. For many, this seems like basic common sense. It's how residential real estate is bought and sold, and properties are leased. For some, it's simply a differentiator from the competition. But in my years with SVN , it has made me realize that it's bigger than incentivizing demand for a client property. In fact, our shared fee and the collaborative philosophy behind it, carries over into our many other services. That's because it's very simple collaborating with the entire industry to create value for clients is a win-win strategy. Here's how it works:

1. Sharing fees puts clients' needs first. It's a story that no other firm can tell. And, this is one of the many ways that we create amazing value with our clients.
2. Sharing fees encourages collaboration within and across all SVN offices, and also throughout the much larger real estate community. It's the reason people like to do business and work with SVN Advisors. This is how we create amazing value with our colleagues.
3. Sharing fees facilitates opportunities for all markets, no matter what size. It allows our decision makers to remain local to and engaged in the cities and towns where they live and work. This is how we create amazing value with our communities.
4. Sharing fees brings transparency to the process. Transparency builds trust, encourages inclusivity and tears down barriers to entry. This is how we create amazing value for all.

But the sharing and transparency do not begin and end with our property listings. We also represent tenants and users of space. Since our founding in 1987, we have evolved into a full-service commercial real estate brand covering all asset classes. Our origins are in landlord/owner services and while Sales, Leasing and Property Management make up the majority of our services, our occupier/user services have been thriving and today round out our real estate platform. And, while sharing fees is our hallmark, when we represent our clients we share SVN resources in order to create the best real estate experience for them. When it comes to representing users, we recognize that tenants' space needs are changing because we, ourselves, are changing. Today we have asset classes merging, new creative class tenants emerging and the once-separate "work-live-play" concepts all converging. As our clients change, we too will adapt, and we will always collaborate across offices and specialties in order to create amazing value with our clients, colleagues and communities.

Another big differentiator for SVN is that we are a franchise operation. When we first launched our franchise operations, we were hesitant to broadcast that we were franchising the SVN brand and system. Yet our franchise owners have come to realize that this is the best way to combine global, firm-level service with local decision-making and the opportunity for our owners to be entrepreneurial. Franchising done well can empower small, medium, and large business enterprises, while allowing managing directors and their advisors the independence to be true business owners. Although it presents unique challenges on our end at SVNIC, it's been a successful way to grow the brand with like-minded real estate practitioners.

Finally, you will see mention of a shared value Network throughout the book. While we share a similar acronym, our brand name derives from our history and founding, but our culture embraces the shared value philosophy. At SVNIC, we are huge proponents of inclusive recruiting and expansion. As you will learn, this is not just a marketing angle but a long-term strategic growth plan. Shared value refers to a methodology of business growth that benefits society while creating new opportunities for profit. It's not an either/or proposition but rather *yes, and*. When we reference a shared value network, we intentionally include the entire real estate-related community and all those who want to enter into it as clients or colleagues. If we can break down the invisible barriers that prevent non-traditional advisors and clients from working with the commercial real estate industry, we believe that we will see unprecedented profit and growth that will spark the same in our respective communities.

This book outlines the SVN philosophy as envisioned by the SVN leadership team and founder Mark Van Ness. It's also the result of a collective effort by every single SVN Advisor, past and present, who believed in and has lived the SVN Difference. A community is defined as a feeling of fellowship with others that develops as a result of sharing common attitudes, interests, and goals. Here at SVN we are more than a real estate company, business enterprise, or franchise organization – we are a true community, to which we often refer to as our family, and therein lies our competitive advantage.

- **Kevin Maggiacomo,**
  CEO & President, SVN International Corp.

Acknowledgments

Thank you to Mark Van Ness and Kevin Maggiacomo for your leadership, guidance and contributions to the company and this book. Thank you also to George Slusser and Solomon Poretsky for your contributions on our executive team and for adding your voices to this project. Special thanks to our amazing SVN International Corp. (SVNIC) team without whom none of us would make it through the day. Your talent, dedication and outstanding good humor make SVNIC an exciting and fun place to work. And, thank you to our entire SVN® family including our franchise owners, managing directors, Advisors and staff for the outstanding work that you do for your clients and on behalf of the SVN brand each and every day.

The SVN® Core Covenants

A company's core values provide clarity on what is truly important for organizational success, personal and professional conduct and what to expect from each other. At SVN, our Core Covenants express our values and culture, and differentiate us from the competition.

1. Create amazing value with my clients, colleagues and community.
2. Cooperate proactively and place my clients' best interests above my own.
3. Include, respect, and support all members of the commercial real estate industry.
4. Honor my commitments.
5. Personify and uphold the SVN brand.
6. Resolve conflicts quickly, professionally and effectively.
7. Take personal responsibility for achieving my own potential.
8. Excel in my market area and specialty.
9. Focus on the positive and the possible.
10. Nurture my career while valuing the importance of family, health and community.

Introduction

Shared Value, Commercial Real Estate and the American Dream

In 2013, Kevin Maggiacomo, CEO & President of SVN International Corp. (SVNIC), gave a TEDx talk about the importance of adding intentionality of purpose to our lives and businesses if we wanted to achieve the American Dream. This was when he introduced the concept of shared value that would prove to be crucial to the SVN® strategic growth plan.

Shared value was originally developed as a concept in 2011 by Harvard Business School professor Michael Porter. Porter defines shared value as: "Policies and operating practices that enhance the competitiveness of a company while simultaneously advancing the economic and social conditions in the communities in which it operates. The concept of shared value—which focuses on the connections between societal and economic progress—has the power to unleash the next wave of global growth."

In other words, shared value is not corporate social responsibility or check-writing philanthropy, instead it combines societal good with a company's economic well-being and advancement. Companies that act with purpose can bolster their profits *and* improve the human experience. The two concepts are not mutually exclusive, as a growing number of companies can attest.

For example, JPMorgan Chase has been steering over $250 million annually into community-building investments like small business development, job-skills training and neighborhood revitalization including creating a "service corps" of advisors in cities that have lost manufacturing jobs. Novartis is trying to effect change in drug pricing by creating lower cost biosimilar drugs, and matching health care costs with patient outcomes. These are not the only examples. At business conferences across the world we are starting to hear about the triple bottom line: people, planet and profits.

While many companies across multiple sectors are only now talking the talk, here at SVNIC we started walking the walk in 2013. Following Kevin's TEDx Talk, our franchisees, Advisors and staff have all worked together to transform our company's culture. Today, SVN offices have become advocates for the deliberate inclusion of women, people of color, veterans, and young people - with or without a college degree - and take steps to ensure their success through equal access to business opportunities for all underrepresented groups. At SVNIC, being inclusive is not just about improving our profit sheet, it's as fundamental as promoting and preserving the American Dream. In fact, commercial real estate is a profession built upon the concept of the American Dream. It does not require an expensive degree, because with the right licensing, training, skills, motivation and business platform, individuals can cross socio-economic barriers and create value for themselves, their families and their communities. At SVNIC, we commit to providing our Advisors with the training, resources, tools and support they need to succeed in commercial real estate.

In 2013, on a stage in Orange County, California, Kevin Maggiacomo told us a story of what we need to do to awaken the American Dream both for ourselves and others. For those who have not seen Kevin's talk, we include the text in its entirety below.

Kevin Maggiacomo, TEDx Orange Coast "Theme: Beautiful Minds"

It's Time to Awaken the American Dream

Maria Civita and her husband Antonio, modest winemakers from Itri, Italy, arrived with their six children on Ellis Island in 1915. They built a winemaking business and chased their American Dream. This lasted for about five years when Prohibition abruptly shuttered their doors. Maria Civita and her husband were left as immigrants in a new country without a trade or a way to support their family.

Now, at that time, Italian-Americans, like many other ethnic groups, were viewed as perpetual foreigners ... outsiders ... not part of America's heritage, despite the fact that almost everyone in America had been in a similar situation only a generation or two before.

Maria Civita, the survivor that she was, sought to change that...to reclaim the American Dream for herself and for other Italian-Americans... so she and her husband harvested the small amount of money they had saved and began lending to their peers.

Beginning with these micro-loans, which helped others pursue their own American Dreams, this "outsider" and her family eventually formalized their business, which grew to become one of the largest regional banks in New England.

Maria Civita's story is like many American Dream stories, but for most people today, that's all it is ... a story, maybe even a myth.

Today there are millions of Americans feeling like outsiders in their own country. Outsiders, who are experiencing what feels like a Prohibition on their own American Dreams.

Just read the headlines:

- Manufacturing trades are disappearing.
- The standards of public education, and even the

schools themselves, are crumbling around us.

- Entire cities are going bankrupt.
- We have a whole generation drowning in student debt.

To those experiencing the effects of these crises, the American Dream is more of a nightmare. And as cynical as this may seem, the numbers suggest that the people most likely to believe in the American Dream today are those who have already attained it. The American Dream is for many a nightmare, or at best, in a coma.

So right now, you may be asking yourself, what does this privileged, white, businessman who is clearly living the American Dream, know about the challenges that a woman, immigrant, minority or other outsider faces in achieving the same?

And, the honest answer is… that I know very little.

But I feel compelled to follow the example of that courageous Italian woman, because this amazing woman was Maria Civita Maggiacomo, my great-grandmother.

And so this takes us right to the root cause of this dissolution of the American Dream

The right of every person living in this country to have access to the American Dream has been instilled in my family for generations – yet somehow, I'd forgotten this.

And my wake-up call came very recently during my company's national conference. As I looked at the audience, I saw a sea of people who looked just like me. Nearly all were men. Nearly all were white.

Now, this existed, despite the fact that historically, some of the highest performers in our organization had been women and minorities ... and to the father of a Dominican teenager, whom I adopted at age 6, this disappointed me.

Yet, it occurred to me….

If *I* was unconscious as to how *I* was excluding Americans from a shot at achieving the Dream, then others were probably doing the same ... our beautiful minds had become tragically myopic.

Now, my motivation for tackling this problem isn't rooted solely in my heritage or wanting to help those less fortunate. Excluding people from the American Dream is a big problem for those of us who are living the Dream, as well as for those who are not.

But let's back up a moment: America doesn't hold the rights to the American Dream.

It would be more accurate to describe the vision as the "Human Dream" - right? I mean, the desire to have one's hard work rewarded with a good life for one's family is universal. America earned the right to call the "Human Dream" the "American" Dream by being the one country where people had the best chance for upward mobility.

The sad news today though is that there are at least 14 countries where people have more upward social mobility than in the United States. The "American Dream" should now be called the "Danish Dream" or the "Down Under Dream" or even the "Canadian Dream."

In 1988, the United States was ranked by *The World* magazine as the #1 place in the world to be born when it comes to opportunity. Today, *The Economist* Intelligence Unit has us ranked #16.

Want to know where we rank #1? .... Among rich nations, America, has the highest number of children living in poverty. And as the gap between the "haves" and the "have nots" in the U.S. continues to grow, our upward mobility suffers, the Dream becomes the exception rather than the rule, and society stagnates. And what happens in a stagnant society is that the economy falters and innovation and opportunity are diminished ... for everyone.

To paraphrase Debbe Kennedy, the author of *Putting Our Differences to Work*, "New wealth avenues are almost always created by outsiders ... by people who know little or nothing about the normal way of doing things." People like Maria Civita.

Yet, the irony is that you could argue that my great-grandmother would have more barriers to success today than she had nearly 100 years ago - at a time when, as a woman, she didn't even have the right to vote.

Just because the American Dream has been hijacked by a small portion of our society; doesn't mean we simply give up.

So how do we do this? How do we take action and empower outsiders to innovate and show us the way?

By bringing intentionality to the problem and turning it into an opportunity.

And the first step is recognizing that the dissolution of the American Dream is everyone's problem. What we can't do is sit around waiting for the government or the next great civil rights leader to bring back the Dream.

While you and I may not be able to single-handedly transform the education system for the 21st century, there is one thing every one of us can do that will be a game-changer. And it involves the simple concept of embracing different. What if we each reach out and proactively embrace different people, different ideas, different opportunities?

Now this isn't new. Studies have shown that companies prosper under diversity, and this is in part why I'm proactively seeking out and recruiting qualified people who don't look like me or like the rest of my industry. But not just to check off some Noah's ark version of a company, it's because if they don't look like me, chances are that they don't think like me either and that's where we all benefit.

Diversity + Inclusion = Improved (Business) Outcomes.

Now, you don't have to be the CEO of a company to do this. Anybody can make a difference.

If you're a kid with a rare brittle bone disease resulting in over 70 broken bones before your 10th birthday, you could easily say, "Hey, I'm just a kid with brittle bones, I can't wake anybody up," or you could say, "The world needs a pep talk!" and inspire millions to have a positive attitude on videos that garner 28,000,000 views. If you don't know who Kid President is ... there are 28,000,000 reasons right there why you should.

But you don't have to create a viral video to bring intentionality to reclaiming the American Dream. How about simply taking a look at your social media feeds. Do most of them look like you? Think like you? If they do, then you're only receiving a small sliver of information about what's happening in the world ... reach out to a more diverse crowd.

If you're a woman or a minority in corporate America, you could keep your head down and focus on your job and family, or you could go after leadership roles in your company that give you a voice. And if your company throws up roadblocks, then knock them down ... or keep looking. There are resources out there to help you like Sheryl Sandberg's *Lean In* movement, which is helping thousands of women across the country make an impact.

Or you could raise consciousness like Etsy. In 2012, Etsy's founders realized it was crazy to have only 5% female engineers for a website that mostly caters to women. So, when traditional recruiting didn't work to increase that number, they sponsored a Hacker School Program that provided female engineers with scholarships and they ended up recruiting 50% women engineers without lowering hiring standards.

In each of these examples, we see intentionality. We see individuals expanding their own American Dream by finding innovative ways to offer the Dream to others through inspiration, a leg up, leadership, or an opportunity.

I bet if we all look back, we each have a Maria Civita in our family. Someone who wouldn't let even a national Prohibition destroy their American Dream. Someone who helped reclaim the dream for others.

It's time we all got back to doing the kinds of things that will bring back the true American Dream, which is not "I've got mine" but rather -- opportunity for everyone regardless of circumstances or birthright.

I'm not just challenging myself, but I'm challenging you, too. Let's put our beautiful, diverse and innovative minds together and awaken the American Dream from its coma. I'm asking you today to take that next step. Embrace different. Lend a hand or even an inspiration. Share the stage. Stick your neck out, especially … especially when you don't have to. Because that's all part of living the American Dream. A dream that is well worth living."

* * *

As Kevin explains, being inclusive is a growth strategy, and it is a key to bringing the American Dream back for everyone. I want to emphasize that at SVN we are not focused on attracting diverse professionals to the brand at the expense or instead of our more traditional members of the commercial real estate industry. Inclusivity is a strategy in *addition* to traditional growth strategies, and intended to benefit everyone. This is especially needed now, when in the U.S. we are facing a coming talent crisis as baby boomers start to retire. Due to the recession, millennials, who now make up the majority of the U.S. labor force, are all too scarce in commercial real estate. Add to this a student debt crisis that has wiped out a large portion of our traditional talent pipeline. A commercial real estate brokerage career is lucrative, but it's commission-based. Millennials and Generation Z cannot pursue commission-based job opportunities if they are burdened with student debt.

While the pool of talent is shrinking, we have nearly two-thirds of the commercial real estate brokerage industry on the cusp of retirement. We are facing an imminent brain drain at the same time we need to broaden our talent base to look more like our client base, which is the rest of the U.S. and the world at large.

Commercial real estate touches everything and everyone, and it's simply not good business to maintain a closed network in a global society where data and information is becoming more transparent and commoditized. As a result, SVN has become a brand with a purpose not just because it's the right thing to do for our clients, colleagues and communities; it's also good business and a strategy that will best position us for continued success, growth, and influence in both the near- and long-term.

That's our vision. Now let me tell you, with a little help from our entire leadership team, the rest of the story of how the SVN brand's unique culture developed, and how it is the key to our becoming one of the fastest growing and innovative brands within the commercial real estate industry.

Chapter One

A Brief History of How We Got from There to Here

Over the years, the Commercial Real Estate (CRE) industry has evolved in fits and starts, often being more reactionary than proactive, and preferring the comfort of the status quo over the risks of innovation. The *"if it ain't broke don't fix it"* mentality generally trumped any *"nothing ventured, nothing gained"* efforts. But every industry has upstarts willing to push the envelope, and that's where the SVN® family tree starts.

In 1987, Mark Van Ness left a successful brokerage and regional management career at a national company to start a new kind of brokerage called Sperry Van Ness (now SVN International Corp.). The vision was to create a more effective system through the elimination of practices that reduce market value for the sole purpose of double-ending transactions. Keeping both sides of a transaction inside a single brokerage is a common practice in CRE because it allows the broker to keep the full commission. While less prominent in tenant-landlord representation, the majority of CRE firms focused on investment sales consider it financially expedient and to this day, continue to limit the exposure of their clients' properties.

SVN Advisors bucked that exclusivity trend, and as a result we were one of the first CRE brands to champion broker cooperation, meaning the company worked with competing agents to market, sell, and lease properties. Of note is our unique use of the title "Advisors" for our brokers. We adopted this moniker early on because a "broker" focuses on the asset or the transaction. In contrast, an "advisor" focuses on creating value for clients, even if that means advising them not to make a particular transaction or list a particular asset.

From the very beginning, the company mandate was not just to think outside the box, but to think about the box itself and transform services offered by traditional CRE firms by adding an advisory dimension that creates the most value for clients. The goal was to create unprecedented value for commercial real-estate investors. The founders believed transparency, cooperation, and collaboration were integral to achieving that goal. Over the next thirty years, the company would revolutionize the CRE services business, and change the future of commercial real estate, by being a brand with a point of view and a strong differentiating value proposition.

From the beginning, SVNIC was an aggressive early adopter on the technology front. In the early 1990s, it was the first brokerage to leverage local area networks, connecting all its advisors together via an internal system to foster better collaboration and expand marketing power.

In 2000, the company developed an online publishing system with remote access—a decade before the cloud became a household term. Pioneering a single point of entry software fundamentally changed the way Advisors created, generated, marketed, and completed CRE transactions. Those innovative virtual operations systems earned the SVN brand several RealComm Digie awards and inspired the creation of numerous other third-party online publication products and companies. Technology was the foundation for SVN's national expansion, and making it the fastest-growing firm in commercial real estate, adding 125 offices and one thousand Advisors over a six-year span.

In 2002, SVNIC became the only national firm to house an in-company auction division. Believing that maximum competition equals maximum value, the transparent nature of a "list-to-close in 90 days" auction product was a perfect fit with the company's vision and philosophy. Within a decade, SVN Advisors started leveraging online bidding platforms.

In 2003, the company added landlord and tenant representation, and property and asset management services. That same year, SVNIC began its transformation into a national franchise operation, which gave managing directors ownership of local company brokerages. It was a win-win for both clients and company, combining a local business perspective with national resources.

In 2008, the economy turned and the company—and the entire real estate industry—was hit by lightning. Volume in the industry dropped 90 percent in one year. Fortunately, in late 2007, Mark Van Ness had called for a complete infrastructure revamp. The challenge was to restructure enough to be sustainable with only 20 percent of the volume. Many on the executive team considered it impossible.

A strategy document from that time called for the company to position itself today for leadership tomorrow and develop profitability tools for our franchisees. The 2007 SVN executive team sat down with a blank slate to set up the company to achieve these goals. They understood that they essentially needed to start a new company, as if the old one had gone out of business. They made some tough decisions in late 2007, yet succeeded in developing a sustainable business, rebuilt on a scalable infrastructure and focused on providing profitability products that gave SVN Advisors an edge in the field. The new plan also positioned the company to be stable in any market.

Until that point, SVNIC had been operating the franchise business in the shadows of the corporate stores, when in reality these were two distinctly different businesses. In 2008, SVNIC sold off the corporate stores, and restructured the business around the franchise operations. This would allow the brand to not only weather the Great Recession but provide for permanent sustainability by creating a new way of operating the business and a new platform to promote fresh and innovative ideas.

The Great Recession heralded other changes. In 2010, Mark Van Ness fully retired and the baton was passed to Kevin Maggiacomo, our current CEO and president. Kevin had started at SVNIC in 2001, where he helped facilitate the national expansion and worked his way up to vice president of the franchise business and chief operating officer before being appointed president in 2008.

By 2009, Kevin's primary role was focused on engaging the stakeholders by creating a culture of collaboration. Implementing that strategy was done though regular communication with office leaders and their Advisors, getting to know their clients, selling a point of view, evangelizing about the brand, and generally, leading by example. Knowing full well that some of the best ideas had come from the SVN Advisor base, Kevin took a disciplined approach to leveraging their input. From 2009 through today, Kevin has continued this practice and taken on the responsibility to ensure that our unique culture is preserved, to encourage outside the box thinking, capitalize on intellectual assets, and allocate resources to maintain the company's mission and vision.

In 2013, Kevin and his leadership team, of which I was now a part, began another aggressive rebuild, investing heavily in growth, launching training products, and embarking on an international expansion. In 2015, after two years of laying the groundwork, we officially changed our brand name to SVN to better reflect who we are today—a purpose-driven company committed to generating profitable revenue while simultaneously improving the industry, society, and our communities. Today, we also offer more services across more asset classes, including sales, leasing property management, tenant representation, and corporate real estate services.

While we shortened our name, we updated our icon. We believe the new name better represents the company's stakeholders. However, we kept facets of our original three-building logo by morphing the building into three brand pillars that represent openness, inclusiveness, and innovation. These three brand pillars are a large part of the SVN Difference. We also encircled the pillars with rings that represent the entire real estate environment ecosystem of which we are a part.

The history of the SVN brand is one informed by innovation. When launched in 1987, it was a functional brand that also had a point of view. Mark Van Ness, as a founder, had recognized the inefficiencies, conflicts of interests, and institutional dysfunction of the commercial real estate investment sales world. He built a company designed to put clients' interest first, which simultaneously proved profitable for SVNIC and all our franchisees.

Fast forward to today, and realize that what we have created in our brand over time, over the hundreds of thousands of transactions, and through our Advisors, is trust—among the brokerage community, our peers, and our competitors. Having worked at other regional and national commercial real estate firms, where locked doors, locked drawers, and internal competition for clients was the norm, I was surprised to see something completely different at SVN. Collaboration was not just a statement on the company's website, it was ingrained in the culture.

Throughout the rest of this book you will learn more of how the SVNIC leadership team, along with every single one of our SVN managing directors and Advisors, have created a culture and a company built for growth, sustainability and greatness for decades to come.

The SVN® Brand Timeline

1987 The Sperry Van Ness® brand was founded in Orange County, CA, on the principle of compensated cooperation.

1990 Expands to new offices and becomes the first commercial brokerage to connect all agents and offices.

1995 Gains #1 market share in apartment and shopping center sales in Southern California.

2000 Launches virtual brokerages under the Sperry Van Ness brand in Central and Northern California; license model launched in limited manner.

2001 Develops a virtual online tracking system for properties.

2007 Becomes the fastest growing brand in

commercial real estate.

2008 Transforms to a pure franchise system.

2009 Expands services to leasing; adds product specialties.

2011 Launches property management.

2012 Launches corporate real estate services.

2013 Expands to 170 offices.

2014 Begins international expansion.

2015 Officially changes name to SVN®.

2017 Expands to more than 200 offices in 6 countries.

2019 Participates in total transaction volume of over $12.3 billion.

Chapter Two

Creating a Culture of Trust that Lasts

In 2017, 30 years after the founding of SVN International Corp. (SVNIC), Kevin Maggiacomo, CEO & president, gave his annual state of the company address in Tampa, Florida and spoke of the connection between then and now.

"In 1987, SVN® was launched as a functional brand, but a brand with a point of view.

And in thinking about conversations I've had with Mark Van Ness over the years, about the inspiration for launching SVN – and you've heard it, empirically – he recognized the tremendous inefficiencies, conflicts of interests and dysfunctional state of the commercial real estate investment sales world. The commercial real estate industry is fraught with brokers' interest-first behavior. He sought to change all of that and to put clients' interest first. This resulted in a business model designed to simultaneously place client interests first and still be good for SVN's bottom line.

"These conversations always get me thinking ... that there is something incredibly timely, current and leading edge with respect to the SVN Difference, even though that differentiating value proposition was born 30 years ago. In a recent discussion with our Chief Operating Officer Diane Danielson, she distilled it down to something very timeless and simple, yet eye-opening: That what we have created in this brand over time, over hundreds of thousands of transactions, and throughout the SVN Advisor base, is trust.

- Trust - In operating with an organizationally-leveraged business model geared towards proactively cooperating with the brokerage community, using one-half of the fee as an incentive to ensure maximum value for a seller's property.
- Trust - Amongst our peers and competitors, who can independently access our inventory and know that they can rely on one-half of the fee and a paycheck if they work on and successfully put a buyer into one of our listings.
- Trust - Because we do all of the above proactively.

"Today, having a "trust-ability" mindset - as business author Don Peppers says - is critical. Businesses today must make their actions more transparent, honest, and less self-interested. Only those companies who design their business models purposefully, so as to ensure that whatever's best for the client or customer is financially better for the firm, overall. And that sounds precisely like the mindset that was in place in 1987 and still defines SVN today.

"Running against this SVN competitive advantage - which you might not think about very often - lies an implosion of trust. The 2017 Edelman Trust Barometer reveals that trust is in crisis around the world and the general population's trust in many key areas, of which businesses are one, are at all-time lows. According to Edelman's global survey, less than 50% of consumers trust the businesses in their environments. In the commercial real estate services industry, which is still largely mired in outdated thinking, locked doors and drawers, I have to believe that it, too, would face some pretty low trust scores. Un-trustable business models thrive in commercial real estate brokerage today largely because being un-trustable can be highly profitable, at least in the short term and that term may be getting even shorter.

"And so my message here is the following. First, trust, in an increasingly chaotic political and corporate environment, is being demanded and will soon separate those companies that are built to last. Second, our SVN business model is designed to place the client's interests first - even when we don't have to - to ensure a better outcome for the client. As a result, SVN is positioned to earn the highest degree of "trust-ability." Third, for 30 years we have been building an industry-wide value interconnected system by always sharing inventory, commissions, and information, resulting in an unprecedented reputation of trust and fair-dealing.

Our competitors know that they can rely on and trust SVN for half the fee if they put a buyer into one of our listings. And this practice spills over into all of our other services. We do things right, do the right thing, and do both proactively. In short, honesty as a competitive advantage.

"We are a business. A purpose-driven business. It's our commitment to create economic value from our core values. Our values are simple. We believe that wealth and success are driven by sharing and collaborating with our clients, colleagues and even our competitors. We also believe that the greatest economic opportunities arise from being inclusive and having healthy and thriving communities that we have a shared responsibility to build. We further believe that we are at a unique time in economic history when we can fully power-up our shared values to become an incredible revenue generating machine, through creating new value for our clients, colleagues and communities. Our history is a story about three decades of forward-thinking individuals, courageous decisions, technological innovations, and a cultural awareness that have left SVN's indelible fingerprints throughout the industry. And we're far from done. Our latest strategies, initiatives, and expansions are designed to ensure that SVN will continue to impact—and lead—the commercial real estate industry well into the foreseeable future."

* * *

As Kevin spoke on stage, I looked across the audience, made up of hundreds of our SVN managing directors and Advisors, and the concept of "trust-ability" resonated with me. It complements our SVN mission statement and affirms my own experience that trust is one of those intangibles—along with purpose—that sets the SVN brand apart.

Chapter Three

The SVN® Core Covenants

Covenant: an agreement that is usually formal, solemn, and intended as binding.

The SVN® Core Covenants are the heart and soul of the SVN brand and have become the company's indispensable and lasting tenets. They define a code of behavior that describes what is and what is not acceptable. Our company's core values are designed to promote organizational success by stressing personal integrity, professional responsibility, transparency, inclusivity and accountability to each other. They also reflect how our culture differentiates us from the competition.

Our core covenants create a positive working environment for the entire SVN community. All our

Advisors agree to abide by these core covenants while upholding our brand.

Early on in the company's history, no one wrote down these values because SVN Advisors were living them every day in a single office with the whole management team within arms' reach of each other. Then, SVN expanded outside of Southern California, opened additional offices, and recruited new managers to run each location. Growth meant increased distance, and it was quickly apparent that the culture of each office was developing differently and did not necessarily convey the SVN company values.

To preserve SVN's unique culture, the company's founders convened in order to document the company's values, and the original SVN core covenants were established. They have since been updated, but have survived for decades, virtually intact:

1. Create amazing value with my clients, colleagues and community.
2. Cooperate proactively and place my clients' best interests above my own.
3. Include, respect, and support all members of the commercial real estate industry.
4. Honor my commitments.
5. Personify and uphold the SVN brand.
6. Resolve conflicts quickly, professionally and effectively.
7. Take personal responsibility for achieving my own potential.
8. Excel in my market area and specialty.
9. Focus on the positive and the possible.
10. Nurture my career while valuing the importance of family, health and community.

Today, these core covenants enhance our culture of collaboration, attract like-minded professionals to our local offices, and also help resolve disputes. They are the basis of our competitive advantage. We're so committed to them that we require our managing directors to agree in writing that they will lead and live by the core covenants in everything they do with and for SVN so that they may create and nurture a positive working environment and perform as a team member with accountability, responsibility and authority.

Throughout the year at our SVN Jumpstart live training programs, Kevin Maggiacomo gives a presentation about our core covenants. Below are excerpts that explain what the core covenants mean to him and to the SVN brand.

"It might sound like a cliché, but the SVN culture needs to be experienced to be appreciated. During my years with SVN, time and again I've seen internal—and external—disputes resolved promptly and satisfactorily for both parties. I've watched Advisors achieve positive results for their clients as well as colleagues, competitors, and the community through the same transaction. I'm proud of that.

"Successful businesses build their teams on core values. We follow SVN's core covenants to guide our culture, growth, and futures.

"All the core covenants serve a specific business and social purpose. For example, the second on the list—*cooperate proactively and place my clients' best interests above my own*—speaks to the commitment SVN advisors have to serving their clients' interests. That promise instills tremendous confidence in our clients that our priority is them, not simply maximizing fees. Through our covenants, we agree to put our money where our mouths are.

"*Include, respect, and support all members of the commercial real estate industry* states our commitment to evolve along with our client base, in order to better represent those clients in the market. It's about our recruiting and developing leaders from 100 percent of the population. It's about recognizing that diversity of race, gender, and thought is the engine of innovation and productivity. At SVN we have a deep commitment to diversity and inclusion. Not to give back, or to be philanthropic, but to generate more profitable revenue than we otherwise could while creating amazing benefits for all of society's stakeholders.

"*Honor my commitments* sounds obvious, but it's easy to forget to follow up with a client; it's easy to fail to circle back with a relationship you've formed. At SVN, a sure way to increase the likelihood of being brought into a deal, receiving a referral, or being invited in to a pitch, is to become engaged. An equally sure way to develop a negative personal brand is to not return phone calls or not making an introduction you promised.

"*Resolve conflicts quickly, positively, and effectively.* Disputes happen. Healthy debate is encouraged, but disputes between Advisors, competitors, and clients are expensive in both time and money. A commitment to quickly and effectively resolve disputes benefits all parties, not to mention that you will likely need or want to do business with that broker, that seller, that buyer in the future so resolution prevents a burned bridge.

"*Focus on the positive and the possible.* Visualize where you want to be, and emotionally commit yourself to taking the actions and making the decisions and communicating in a way that will achieve the result.

"*Nurture my career while valuing the importance of family, health, and community.* We always preach the importance of work-life balance. Yes, it takes discipline, organization, and elimination of the wasted time we all spend on activities, thoughts, and distractions that don't positively contribute to our lives. But a balanced life supports a successful career and a successful family. The SVN way is to value both so that we may excel in both areas.

"Our culture at SVN is deeply rooted in and is inextricably tied to productivity. Our culture does make for good recruiting and marketing, but more than that, it makes for good business."

* * *

Clients want to work with professionals whom they trust. Advisors from all backgrounds want to work at companies that create opportunities. And our communities want firms who are committed to improving where they live, work and play. This is why we stand by our SVN® Core Covenants - because they make all of this possible.

Chapter Four

SVN® Training, Innovation, and Technology

An integral element of the SVN® culture is our embrace of technology and training to facilitate value and productivity. On the technology front, we've always been cutting-edge thought leaders, ahead of the curve in the commercial real estate industry. When we combine this with our training, we create a powerful platform for our managing directors and Advisors. In the early 1990s, we became the first brokerage firm to leverage local area networks, connecting all of our advisors together via a single system to foster and generate greater collaboration and marketing power.

In 2000, SVN International Corp. (SVNIC) revolutionized the commercial real estate business by developing a remote, online server-based publishing system. In 2002, SVN became the only national firm with an in-company auction division. Ten years later, we started leveraging online bidding platforms through a series of multi-state, multi-property online auction events.

In 2010, we moved to the Google platform, and a short time later made a commitment to harness the power of social media, becoming one of the first commercial real estate brands to leverage that space. SVN clients wanted unfettered access to their Advisors across multiple media, and we were able to give them exactly what they were asking for through our expansive technology platform. This is not to say it was a smooth and easy transition, because we operate in an industry that is especially reluctant to embrace technology.

Pushing the commercial real estate industry forward with technology has always been a personal challenge for me. From 1999 to 2003, I was on a mission to convince real estate professionals in Boston that email and websites were not fads. It took a while to get everyone on board then, and evolution still remains difficult in this industry. Why is it so hard? Because there are still brokers in the U.S. who practice real estate using just a phone and their Rolodex®, thanks to decades of building strong relationships. However, when the baby boomers retire in the next five to ten years, we will see widespread tech adoption by the remaining Gen Xers, millennials, and the first wave of Generation Z. Here at SVNIC, we are watching the trends and regularly updating our technology and training.

Perhaps the greatest example of how our business practices have evolved to incorporate technology is how we promote our clients' properties. One of the hallmarks of the SVN system is SVN | Live®, our weekly national sales meeting that is simultaneously broadcast to all 200+ offices and open to the entire real estate industry. New and featured properties, represented by SVN Advisors, which might have regional, national and even international appeal, are reported on during the broadcast to SVN Advisors, clients, competing brokers, independent investors, and anyone who registers for the meeting via our SVN.com website. We believe in leveraging technology and the transparency of the SVN system to promote our clients' properties as quickly and to as many people in the industry as possible. Because we couple this technology with our shared fee system, brokers from competing organizations are incentivized to join the meeting on behalf of their own clients. We are constantly updating the format and the technology behind this meeting, but its evolution is a typical example of SVN innovation.

SVN | Live began as a Monday morning sales meeting in our single office back in 1987. As the company expanded across the country, offices began connecting telephonically and via webinar thereafter. When I joined in 2012, we moved to an interactive format with slides that we promoted via social media. In 2014, Kevin Maggiacomo and the leadership team decided that if our goal was to create increased demand for our properties we needed to open up the sales call to non-SVN colleagues, clients and potential clients, becoming the first commercial real estate brand to embrace the power of technology-enabled open markets. Recently, we made further investments in the technology and added screen-sharing, re-broadcast and additional updated video capabilities.

In 2014, we launched our SVN System for Growth™ online training platform. Created specifically for SVN Advisors and managing directors by Solomon Poretsky, SVNIC's chief development officer. This, along with our in-person Jumpstart, and additional elite training programs for managing directors and top Advisors, helps our brokers and offices excel in the marketplace. Below Solomon Poretsky describes the philosophy behind our training programs:

"What do clients want? Clients want to work with innovative service providers who work collaboratively to drive results. What does talent want? Talent wants to work collaboratively in an innovative environment. SVN's value proposition for its clients dovetails with the value proposition for new to the business hires. When you add in our highly skilled local management teams and our platform that allows for cross-office collaboration, we become an even more compelling choice.

"SVN also offers a best-in-class training system for new talent. Our offices can leverage our award-winning SVN System for Growth™ online training system to give new hires the basic skills they need to begin building a commercial real estate brokerage advisor career and to continue training senior Advisors and their management teams. We are also the only company to provide online and in-person training for our managing directors through Jumpstart, the SVN System for Growth, and our year-long SVN | Elite program.

SVN | Elite is an intensive, year-long, management skills enhancement program. Through their participation in phone calls, extensive reading, and in highly interactive meetings, participants cover the entire management continuum, learning how to recruit, train and retain high producing Advisors, and how to build dominant offices.

In addition, we offer support to let each office build its own training system, covering the same standardized items. And, in 2018, we offered our first ever Advisor | Elite program. Like the SVN | Elite program for managing directors, this program is instructor, coach, and peer-based, and involves in-person and online meetings.

Finally, our SVN | Jumpstart program is currently the industry's most comprehensive live training program, giving new-to-the-business professionals the coaching they need to take the basic skills that they have acquired through pre-training and perfect them. It's also a great way to become totally immersed in the SVN culture, which is our SVN Difference."

* * *

Today at SVN, we continue to test for, develop and explore new ways to connect our clients' needs and leads with the entire real estate community and to train the best and most resourceful Advisors in the industry. Technology is changing commercial real estate and we intend to change along with it. This is why we're always pushing our training and technology ahead, so that we can push our Advisors accordingly. We have a history of being a little bit ahead of the technology curve, and this started back when SVNIC was a local California company and the internet was just beginning to change how we do business.

Chapter Five

SVN® Core Services and Specialty Practice Areas

SVN International Corp. (SVNIC) began as an investment sales firm. As the company grew and expanded across the country, our offices began to expand their services. Today SVN® Advisors provide Owner/Investor Services (Sales, Leasing, Capital Markets, Property Management, Accelerated Sales) and Occupier/User Services (Tenant Representation and Corporate Real Estate Services). Within these service categories exist specialty service and asset classes including Hospitality (hotels, golf and resorts); Industrial (self-storage, warehouses, manufacturing, distribution); Land (agricultural/timberland, transitional/entitled); Multi-Family (apartment buildings, mobile home parks, single family rental portfolios, affordable housing, senior housing and student housing); Office (traditional, medical, mixed-use); Retail (multi-tenant, shopping centers, restaurants, single tenant investments).

Many of our core services and specialty asset classes have a national/international product council. Advisors from across the country join our SVN Product Councils, which are led by SVN experts in each service and asset class. Each product council functions across geography and operates like a collaborative practice group. Most councils hold monthly or quarterly deal-making and best practices calls. Others join forces to attend conferences and produce marketing materials focused on their specialty. Having these practice specialties led by SVN experts, means that any Advisor can partner with a product specialist and go after and win business. By using the collective SVN product specialty resume and our expansive geographic presence, we are able to meet clients' needs in almost any market. In essence, the existence of these product councils means that no Advisor ever has to turn down business for lack of expertise. They can simply contact an expert via the councils and partner with them to secure the deal.

SVN® CORE SERVICES

Sales

SVN's team of investment sales professionals provide industry-leading execution on the acquisition and disposition of commercial real estate assets. Their thorough understanding of client needs combined with local market experience and product specialty knowledge enables Advisors to accurately value what makes each property unique. Whether acquiring or selling an investment property, SVN's investment specialists view themselves as partners working on the client's behalf throughout the transaction process. The nuances of submarkets, property condition, lease length, tenant quality and current lending markets all factor into sophisticated analysis and valuation of each investment real estate asset. SVN clients benefit from the proper valuation of properties combined with the SVN System for promoting properties to the national and international brokerage community.

Leasing

SVN leasing teams will work on the clients' behalf to set retail, office and industrial buildings apart from their competitors. Knowing the pulse of the leasing market allows SVN Advisors to provide clients with a continually refined strategy for attracting and retaining the most desirable tenants. SVN Advisor goals are client goals – to maximize the building's value by filling it with right mix of tenants.

Capital Markets

The SVN® Capital Markets advisory team is made up of experts in national investment sales, and in debt and equity financing, in all major asset classes. The advisory team is supported by SVN commercial real estate Advisors who have the knowledge, experience and expertise in both local and submarket arenas. Our SVN Advisors understand not only the needs of the institutional buyer, seller and borrower, but also the level of detail and sophistication required to fully market, sell and finance properties from $20 million to $200 million and greater.

Corporate Real Estate Services

SVN corporate real estate specialists serve as the outsourced real estate department for clients with multiple locations in various markets. Our experts provide the strategic real estate advice and planning that corporations need to accomplish their real estate-related goals and maximize overall profit in a cost-effective manner. SVN's Corporate Real Estate Services professionals understand client businesses so that they can lead clients through the process of increasing operating efficiencies, margins and EBITDA (Earnings Before Interest, Taxes, Depreciation and Amortization); strategic portfolio planning; transaction management and reporting; lease administration and project management; implementing global best practices and establishing portfolio stewardship reports.

Tenant Representation

Other commercial real estate brands force you into a category. SVN Advisors understand that today's tenants defy definition. Co-working spaces are locating within retail stores and centers. Medical walk-in clinics are now standard retail tenants. Dentists and dermatologists sell merchandise. Stores are for experiencing products, but ordering is done online. The distinction between asset types is being blurred and even eradicated. This is why when it comes to space, SVN Advisors focus on the experience, not just the square footage.

As members of a fast-growing commercial real estate brand, SVN Advisors understand how crucial a dynamic and transparent real estate experience is to clients. Once engaged, our tenant representation professionals partners with clients to provide the local market expertise and full market access to make a search as efficient as possible. Should clients expand beyond their existing market, our Advisors can work with any of our 200+ offices to provide seamless representation at the SVN level of expertise. With its national account capability—- where Advisors can deliver the information, guidance and negotiation skills necessary to make a move or expansion a long-term success— clients consider the SVN system as an extension of their business.

Property Management

SVN franchisees collectively manage over 50 million square feet of commercial property. This places SVN as one of the top property management brands in the United States.[1] The SVN property management business extends the collaborative model by leveraging national vendor relationships and working closely with leasing and sales teams from across the country. SVN property managers benefit from a service council of experts, a national relationship with the Institute for Real Estate Management (IREM), along with other tools and resources to help their clients reduce their operating expenses.

One unique product that all SVN franchisees who own and/or manage properties have access to is our exclusive master insurance program (MIP). The SVN MIP program uses the collective buying power of SVN Property Management clients throughout the country to provide broad insurance protection at a cost that is generally far below what individual owners could otherwise negotiate on their own. This program has resulted in annual premium savings of 20-40% or more for qualifying clients, while providing owners with broader coverage in many cases.

SVN Advisors know that top quality management is essential for retaining desirable tenants, maintaining strong fiscal management, and ultimately maximizing the long-term value of their clients' investment. That's why SVN teams of property management professionals are prepared and able to offer customized solutions for the operations of client commercial or residential assets. Even if an SVN office does not currently provide third-party property management, it can call upon the expertise of other SVN offices that do provide this service.

---

[1] *Commercial Property Executive* magazine (August, 2017).

Accelerated Sales

Sometimes a property sale is more time-sensitive than price-sensitive. SVN Accelerated Sales professionals and online auctions are able to work with clients who need to move properties sooner rather than later. SVN Accelerated Sales specialists understand timing, market exposure, and valuation needs for each investment real estate asset. This is how they prepare professional marketing campaigns, provide valuation benchmarks based on local market activity, and obtain bids from auction participants to aid clients in achieving client disposition goals.

SVN Advisors provide date-specific sales and special asset solutions. They are an elite group of local and regional auction Advisors located throughout the U.S. and who specialize in areas such as foreclosures, tax sales, multi-properties, receiverships and bankruptcies. SVN Accelerated Sales teams offer the industry's most comprehensive spectrum of auction solutions—from rapid asset resolution and 30-day countdown asset sales to wide area and high impact/high promotion events.

SPECIALTY PRACTICE AREAS

Hospitality

Hotels

Hotel properties are an investment in the available real estate, and in the business that operates the property. This asset class is management and staffing intensive, with quick turnover, sometimes on a daily basis. Due to the short-term nature of the rentals, rates have the ability to change within time periods that can be as short as 24 hours. In addition, they require a large capital investment from investors in order to keep properties in up-to-date conditions that are in line with brand standards.

The quick turnover and flexibility on rates make hospitality properties particularly susceptible to fluctuations in consumer and business spending habits. Investors must analyze historical performance, competing properties, capital needs and location-based demand drivers when considering a new acquisition. These factors create a strong opportunity for hospitality investors to achieve above-average returns through savvy property selection and management. This strength is why the SVN system has Advisors throughout the country who specialize in hotel sales. They help guide sellers and investors through the process from valuation to disposition.

Whether a client is looking to buy or sell in a smaller market, a boutique property, major flagged or unflagged properties, or destination resorts, SVN Advisors can make it happen. Armed with specific knowledge about the factors that impact hospitality properties such as market demographics, competitive property information, average daily rates, occupancy break-even analysis, amenity assessments, and more, SVN Advisors understand how to add value across all aspects of the hospitality property spectrum.

Golf and Resorts

Golf courses and lifestyle resorts continue to attract and captivate millions of regular customers. As a result, they are increasingly becoming a desired investment commodity, gaining the attention of investors on both a national and international level. Characteristics of in-demand golf courses and resorts include those in established neighborhoods with above-average household incomes, low crime and upscale shopping nearby. Beyond good demographics, investors look for a quality physical plant, mature grounds, strong operations, steady historical income, a variety of income sources and a single entity ownership structure.

SVN Golf & Resort specialists understand the drivers of each property's business, or in some cases, businesses. Their expertise allows sellers to properly price their asset prior to bringing it to SVN's system of international, institutional and private capital buyers. A thorough analysis can attract the attention of more buyers and offers value-add strategies for maximizing future cash flow in order to get the most out of each asset.

Industrial

Self-Storage

Storage properties allow individuals and businesses to lease small amounts of space to store their belongings on a short-term basis. Although lease lengths can be flexible, many storage customers opt to store their belongings for an extended period of time. Self-storage properties compliment urban and suburban spaces where the high rent per square foot of residential and office spaces allow for limited storage in existing buildings. They can also serve as the long-term home for recreational equipment and collectibles.

The self-storage industry is continuing to capture the attention of a broader pool of investors due to its ease of management and resilience during economic pullbacks. Demand for storage units increases when someone loses a job or moves into a smaller home. Compared to other product types that rent many small spaces on a short-term basis, self-storage units have an easier turnover, lower maintenance needs and more straightforward management with regular customer interaction. SVN advisors have been leaders in this asset class that is expected to expand based on the shifts in demographics and the pull of more urban settings.

Warehouses, Manufacturing and Distribution

The tenants/users of warehousing, manufacturing and distribution centers form the backbone of the American economy. These buildings are in demand in suburban and urban areas alike. Buildings vary in size, number of tenants, age, construction quality, tenant credit quality, lease length, building use and location. Regardless, the need for storage and production space expands and contracts in step with the economy. Vacancies can sometimes be difficult to fill depending on location and building particulars, but landlords enjoy predictability to their income stream once a multi-year lease has been executed.

Because moving a business is expensive, tenants must find an industrial building with the right ceiling heights, number of loading docks, adequate space for current and future needs and the right location. Well-located buildings will often be near distribution channels such as interstates, railways, ports and airports.

Historically, the industrial market is slow to change. However, changes in our economy such as the growing role of the U.S. in high-tech manufacturing and the re-localization of retail fulfillment, thanks to a desire to shorten delivery times for e-commerce, are making industrial properties one of the most dynamic parts of the commercial real estate world. SVN Advisors work together across markets to stay ahead of the competition and to deliver the best possible results for clients.

Land

Analyzing land to determine its value as

unimproved raw land or its suitability for development requires a thorough understanding of the valuation drivers of each major product type. SVN Advisors will guide astute buyers through site analysis and environmental inspections to determine the site's suitability for a given use. Land values are driven by comparable sales and the extent to which the site could be improved to generate a return for a developer.

Land is a finite resource that has historically tended to rise in value at or above the rate of inflation. Holding costs for raw land are relatively low compared to other product types but the costs can mount up on speculators, developers or investors during short-term down swings in the economy. Exit strategies for land investors typically consist of selling the land for more money to another investor, selling to a developer or developing the land themselves and SVN land experts have the experience and the access to an expanded pool of potential land buyers.

Agricultural/Timberland

As the name implies, agricultural real estate is property, including the land and any associated buildings and structures, which is designated or permitted for the production or cultivation of agricultural products such as fruits, vegetables, livestock, poultry, milk, and eggs. Timberland is property used to cultivate timber. Both types of property are usually classified as rural.

Rural properties generally have at least one acre, and more than 50 percent of the land is vacant (i.e., unoccupied by humans). Also, a property is classified as rural when getting to it requires a dirt or private road.

Agricultural and timberland commercial real estate is specialized, and could include the buying/selling of crop, dairy or horse farms, farming properties, ranches, vacant land zoned for agricultural use, foreclosed farms, and any other agricultural or timber-related business. SVN Advisors across the country work with investors to find the right property for their needs.

Transitional/Entitled

A transitional property is real estate that is in the process of changing from one use to another. For example, a residential property that will become an office. This happens when the original area was zoned for residential use, but has become more commercial and has been re-zoned as such. Transitional properties that are going from residential to commercial may increasing land values.

Entitled land has received all the necessary governmental and regulatory approvals for a particular use. The entitlement process depends on local and state governmental regulations and oversight, and must comply with municipal zoning and future land use. Land must comply with issues including environmental concerns, storm water runoff requirements, connections to off-site utilities, and transport access

When we talk about transitional or entitled properties, we really are focused on zoning and permitted use. It's important for developers or real estate investors to understand what current and future zoning and land use situation is. SVN Advisors who specialize in these properties will be able to guide developers when seeking to find this type of real estate.

Multifamily

Apartment buildings offer homes to America's growing renter population. Rental buildings can range dramatically in size, quality, age, unit mix, construction type and location. Units are generally rented on an annual basis and, for better or worse, tenants often times stay beyond their original lease term. As leases renew, landlords have the ability to increase rents as local market trends dictate. Multi-family assets require dedicated management and regular maintenance of the units, buildings and grounds. Although landlords are not able to pass through most expenses to tenants, many buildings collect additional income streams such as parking, laundry or pet rental income.

Multi-family investors must be closely in tune with their submarket rental competitors and maintain a high management standard for their tenants. Investors looking to make targeted physical improvements to achieve above market rent increases are only limited by the quality and rental rate of new construction multifamily assets in the market. Managers of multifamily assets must be ready to handle quick unit turnovers, occupancy fluctuations, rent collections and frequent tenant interactions.

As this asset class continues to grow to accommodate the demand, our SVN Advisors are reaching outside their local markets through SVN systems including the weekly SVN | Live program to create increased demand and find opportunities for their clients.

Affordable Housing

Affordable multi-family housing rented to tenants is a government-subsidized subset of the existing multifamily inventory. There are many national and local affordable housing programs applicable to rental residential housing. By far, the largest affordable housing programs are LIHTC Section 42, project-based Section 8 and Section 8 vouchers. Affordable housing properties carry additional oversight and regulations from local authorities to insure they maintain compliance in the regulated low-income housing program.

Affordable housing restrictions tied to the rental of units at the property are usually in place on a long-term basis but fixed for a given number of years. Upon expiration of LIHTC Section 42 restrictions or the end of a project-based Section 8 contract, an affordable housing investor must reapply to remain in the program. Shortages of affordable housing in many cities continue to persist. Depending on the property's characteristics and the local submarket, the building may be fully rented with a waiting list or the landlord could have difficulty in finding renters that meet the rental requirements.

The type of asset has very specialized needs, yet our SVN offices have affordable housing experts who team up with local advisors to represent these kinds of properties.

Senior Housing

Senior housing is another subset of the multi-family asset class, and consists of apartments with an age restriction, assisted living facilities, skilled nursing facilities and campuses that include a mix of living options for residents to age in place. Senior housing properties are investments in the real estate as much as they are in the underlying business. As the services and nursing care offered to residents increases so does the need for additional staffing and management. Properties are under the oversight of state regulatory boards and must maintain their license to operate in good standing.

Demand for senior housing is expected to continue to increase as the population ages. Investors should look for properties designed to accommodate seniors, space for necessary building services and room for future building expansion. Top quality assets that generate strong returns are characterized by strong management, desirable demographics and strong historical occupancy. This is a rapidly growing sector of the commercial real estate industry and becoming more and more prevalent within all SVN markets.

Student Housing

As younger generations flood into colleges and universities, demand for student housing continues to grow. While student properties are frequently similar to other apartment buildings, this sub-asset class has unique characteristics. SVN Advisors can help owners navigate issues such as the value of parental co-signatures on leases, deciding between 9- and 12-month lease structures, and handling security deposits with a potentially damage-prone renter base. SVN Advisors can also help investors weigh the risk of competition from on-campus construction and the potential protection for existing assets afforded by communities that may be unwilling to permit additional student housing even when needed.

Single Family Rental Investment Portfolios

With more people renting each year, the industry is experiencing the growth of Single Family Rental Investment Portfolios. A Single Family Rental Investment Portfolio is a collection of 5-5,000 homes owned by a seller that is packaged as a commercial graded cash-on-cash investment. A Build for Rent Investment Portfolio is typically offered by a builder as a portion or entire subdivision of 5-500 homes for sale to a single commercial investor, private capital group or REIT (Real Estate Investment Trust). At SVN, we have experts who specialize in this area and through our expansive geographic reach, we are able to list portfolios from around the country in this fast-growing asset class.

Office

Office (Traditional)

Office buildings typically lease space on multi-year leases to multiple tenants in the form of gross or net leases. Having a large number of tenants in the building reduces the impact felt if any one tenant vacates; however, having more tenants also increases the management responsibility and the likelihood of needing to re-tenant space. Office tenants have specific space needs and filling a vacant space can often be difficult and time consuming. Long-term leases provide tenants and landlords with increased certainty and also lead to higher property valuations.

Each office space and building offers a unique set of characteristics to a tenant. SVN Advisors understand the nuances of each submarket, existing tenant mix, space needs and amenities necessary to create a long-term relationship between tenant and landlord.

Healthcare

In the healthcare property asset class, the real estate serves as the operating space for medical office tenants. Healthcare tenants often require extensive build outs for hospital rooms, clinics, medical labs, and office space. The large capital investment to specialize the use of the building leads to healthcare tenants making long term commitments to the space, whether purchased, developed or leased.

Medical office tenants are not easily replaced but make for desirable tenants due to the long-term predictable cash flow they generate. These tenants seek out modern, accessible buildings that are centrally located with ample parking for clients. SVN healthcare asset experts understand the medical office market and work with both individual owner/operators and investors ranging from family offices to institutions.

Retail

Retail commercial real estate encompasses both small local tenants and large global retailers and can be developed as single tenant locations, street retail, shopping centers, regional malls, or as a crucial part of a mixed-use development. Tenants lease space to serve as the consumer-facing side of their business and only lease the amount necessary for their current needs. Such leases range in structure from gross to triple net and can be short-term or long-term commitments to the location.

Capital investment is necessary to customize each space for a particular tenant's business, but the capital invested for the build-out can also vary widely. Landlords should anticipate regular leasing, management and maintenance costs to keep their investment performing at its peak. Retail investors will experience demand fluctuations for leasing retail space as the economy grows or contracts, but these risks can be mitigated via multi-tenant properties, long-term leases or leasing to tenants with high credit quality.

As e-commerce and demographic changes continue to alter the retail markets, SVN Advisors use their collective expertise to help investors and tenants find the right value when it comes to retail real estate.

Multi-Tenant/Shopping Centers

Shopping centers range in size from a small strip mall with a handful of retail stores, to the larger grocery-store anchored shopping centers common in suburbia, to the multi-anchor malls that are home to a mix of retail, office, restaurant, and even hospitality tenants.

This asset class varies according to the market where

it is located. Some markets may have several abandoned or under-leased strip malls, and others have large, busy malls. In other words, the key factor for investors or tenants looking to find the right multi-tenant property is location. Other factors affecting the viability of multi-tenant shopping centers include the area's income and unemployment rates, crime index, and other demographics. SVN Advisors have the specialized knowledge to help both owners and tenants choose the right property.

Restaurants

Restaurants are one of the best ways to improve a neighborhood. They provide jobs at all levels and can attract both local and out-of-area customers. SVN restaurant specialists provide high-level services to clients in this category including restaurants, nightclubs, taverns, bakeries, caterers, hotels, food processors, and manufacturers. We have industry experts who assist clients in all of the following areas: site search and selection, tenant representation, landlord representation, marketing, business sales and acquisitions.

Single Tenant Net Lease Investments

Retail, office, industrial and special use properties can all be structured as a single tenant lease of the entire building on a net basis, meaning the tenant pays for all or most of the building expenses. This attractive business model allows the tenant to have control of paying the actual operating costs, dramatically lowering the accounting necessary for the investor, making the net income generated for the investor very reliable. Such lease structures often are on a long-term basis and may include renewal options.

Single tenant net leased assets are continuing to grow in popularity with investors seeking predictable income within the real estate industry, and are a favorite asset class to use in 1031 tax-deferred exchanges. Owner/users also will consider a single tenant net leased structure for selling their real estate to an investor and leasing it back on a long-term basis so that the cash tied up in the real estate can be reinvested into growing their business.

Due to the popularity of these assets SVN Advisors use the SVN systems including the weekly SVN | Live program and the single tenant net lease product council to advertise properties to the entire brokerage community. Due to this proactive marketing of our clients' properties, SVN has become a market dominator in the single tenant investment arena. Sharing fees and exposing our listings to the entire brokerage community separates us from the competitors and allows all buyers to compete on a level playing field

* * *

As product types evolve and combine, clients' needs will change and SVN is prepared to change along with them. Due to our local market presence, which is connected and supported by global resources, we are able to work in all asset classes across all markets. This is yet another one of the reasons the SVN Difference is an advantage for our clients.

Chapter Six

The SVN® Difference

In 2013, a year after I joined the SVN® leadership team, we produced an animated video that reflected our mission statement, and our belief in collaboration within a commercial real estate market that is segmented, fragmented, and dysfunctional. The commercial real estate business operates in an environment where the listing broker controls the flow of information to potential buyers, which discourages competition, reduces eyeballs on listings, creates fewer offers, and often causes a property to sell for less than market value. In the instance where the listing brokers do share information, they often refuse to share the commission, leaving absolutely no incentive for buy-side brokers to show the listing to their pool of buyers.

This happens because that's the way the industry is designed. Listing brokers make more money when they procure both the buyer and the seller, even if the client doesn't receive the highest price for their property. Further, brokers have little incentive to maximize the value of a property.

This is not the way free markets are supposed to function, nor is it in the best interest of clients and investors. SVN wants to transform the commercial real estate (CRE) industry into a more functional, efficient ecosystem that benefits everyone, including our own Advisors who profit from increased deal flow, shorter transaction times, and repeat business by satisfied clients.

For over thirty years, SVN has approached commercial real estate differently. We didn't just think outside the box; we reimagined the box and transformed the services offered by traditional CRE firms to create the most value for clients. One of those transformative practices that has given SVN a proven track record of increasing demand for properties is collaboration, which we define as harnessing the power of wide, horizontal networks of participants forming a market to achieve better results.

As outlined above, this collaborative approach is part of what we call the SVN Difference. It's about maximizing value for clients—always. Collaboration is not limited to property listings; the SVN Difference informs every facet of SVN's organization and services. It addresses what we believe is one of the biggest challenges facing the CRE industry: the outdated, opaque, and inefficient broker's-interest-first approach to real estate.

In both strong and weak markets, most CRE brokers still do not proactively market their listings through the brokerage community; instead, they choose to find buyers for their listings in their own databases. That results in significantly reduced competition for assets, which doesn't do much for the seller; however, the practice nets the broker a significantly higher fee. SVN was founded with a purpose: to make the industry more efficient and beneficial for Advisors and their clients. Working to create change—among our associates, within our communities, and especially in our industry—remains our biggest challenge.

Today that original purpose of collaboration has morphed into a shared value goal that encompasses all of our services from Sales, Leasing and Institutional Capital Markets to Accelerated Sales/Auction, Property Management, Tenant Representation and Corporate Real Estate Services. The SVN Difference looks through the lens of collaboration to create the most value for the most stakeholders. To truly embody the SVN Difference, one needs to understand the power of a shared value network. As mentioned earlier, shared value is when you create the most value for the most people through collaboration and intentionality. While monetary value is an integral component, shared value also incorporates societal values and social purposes. When we talk about a shared value network in commercial real estate, we are referring to the entire real estate community as part of that network. We are looking beyond our SVN family of offices, managing directors and Advisors, to include the betterment of all who participate in the commercial real estate industry.

In an article for the *Harvard Business Review,* economist Michael Porter noted: "Capitalism is an unparalleled vehicle for meeting human needs, improving efficiency, creating jobs, and building wealth. But a narrow conception of capitalism has prevented business from harnessing its full potential to meet society's broader challenges. The opportunities have been there all along but have been overlooked. Businesses acting as businesses, not as charitable donors, are the most powerful force for addressing the pressing issues we face.

"The purpose of the corporation must be redefined as creating shared value, not just profit *per se*. This will drive the next wave of innovation and productivity growth in the global economy. It will also reshape capitalism and its relationship to society. Perhaps most important of all, learning how to create shared value is our best chance to legitimize business again."

Porter's article certainly touched a nerve with both Mark Van Ness and Kevin Maggiacomo. Porter's idea was that businesses should generate shared value by creating societal value and benefits through their business activities. This was a separate issue from charitable activities. A company's activities to improve its environment creates shared value. As Porter said, "The success of every company is affected by the supporting companies and infrastructure around it."

Shared value is an evolution of conscious capitalism, which is based on four main principles: 1) Having a higher purpose that engages and inspires employees and customers; 2) shifting from the traditional *shareholder* orientation to a more all-inclusive *stakeholder* orientation that focuses on the best interests of employees, customers, suppliers, investors, and communities; 3) conscious leadership that inspires people and guides them with a common vision; and 4) a conscious culture, where a common set of values connect people to create a productive work environment.

At SVN, we have long embraced the idea that business can be both profitable and a force for good in society. In fact, business can be more profitable as a force for good. In many ways, the commercial real estate industry is often self-serving. As a company and a brand, SVN rebelled against this self-serving mentality. Instead, we are a successful, purpose-driven business committed to creating economic value stemming from our core values. When we shortened our name and brand to SVN, we were not just embracing the ease of an acronym (and a valuable three-letter URL), we were acknowledging our role as part of a true shared value network that encompassed the entire commercial real estate ecosystem and as a result we could both elevate returns and society by creating value for all. So yes, at SVN we *are* different. Moreover, we are successful in large part because we are different. Our participation in and dedication to a shared value network that involves our clients, competitors and communities is about embracing our differences.

When we say that we're built to create amazing value for our clients, colleagues and our communities, what we're saying is that our success comes from the success of everyone and every community we touch. It comes from creating opportunities for a diverse pool of applicants, encouraging more people to experience the life-changing opportunities of a career in commercial real estate than at any other firm, and bringing those values back to benefit our local communities.

Shared value is part of our corporate brand (the part of our brand that is client-facing) and is also a huge part of our employment brand for recruiting. Bringing intentionality to recruiting, training and developing women and minorities is a shared value growth strategy implemented not to be philanthropic, but because it is a strategic advantage in an aging workforce. We will discuss our employment brand strategy in the next chapter, for now let's focus on our communities.

Shared Value and Our Communities

We often think of shared fees as the SVN Difference, but - as our mission statement says - our goal is to "create amazing value with our clients, colleagues and communities." How do we create shared value for our communities? We do this by using the power of our real estate businesses to improve the communities in which we live and work.

Each SVN office is independently owned and operated, with vested ties to its community. Many of these communities struggle with pockets of higher than average unemployment, a lack of affordable housing, and other social challenges. While government and private organizations should play a part in solving such issues, we believe a big part of the solution to the social problems that exist in our communities lies in the power of capitalism, in the private sector, and in the shared value networks that can connect them all. This isn't just wishful thinking. We regularly see examples of this from our SVN offices.

Take a look at one of our top annual producing Advisors working in Maryland who became aware of an abandoned, former pharmaceutical facility. Originally used for researching and producing poultry vaccinations before the company moved on, the old building, which had been built in 1960, was no longer serving a purpose in our franchisee's community. The Advisor aggressively marketed the property to the commercial real estate brokerage community and to residential brokers. One of those residential brokers was a member of a local church that was looking for a new location. The church repurposed some of the property to serve as the church's campus and then converted the property frontage into three commercial lots that were leased to retailers and a restaurant, which in turn brought jobs back to the community. And the SVN Advisor? Well, he earned a six-figure commission from creating shared value for his community.

Our team in Chicago developed an expertise in

restaurants, which are a popular retail investment and a crucial component of local economies. It is the single best commercial use of a property if the goal is to revitalize a neighborhood because it provides a wide variety of employment opportunities. At the same time it also capitalizes on the millennial experiential retail trend. It can be a win for all stakeholders from the community to the investors.

Another franchisee sold a former feed mill in Delaware that had been vacant for years by creatively going out of his market and targeting potential tenants in industries that could leverage and repurpose the farming infrastructure. He succeeded and the new tenant, a manufacturer, created twenty-five jobs in a small town, positively impacting the lives of its residents.

These are but a few of the examples of the SVN culture in action. They demonstrate the power of a shared value strategy addressing social issues within a business context, creating benefits for both business and society while creating revenue. In 2018, we launched the SVN Communities Fund. This fund will provide grants for our most loyal and productive offices to use for local community improvement projects. We believe that our local owners can create shared value within their own communities and that's a difference we can stand behind and support.

While not every transaction will be a win-win for all, at SVN, our Advisors are using the shared value strategy throughout their own networks to broker deals that contribute to a community's sense of place, making the area better for everyone. That sits at the heart of our SVN culture.

Chapter Seven

The SVN® Employment Brand and Gender Balance

Business demographics are changing around the globe. Commercial real estate needs to better represent our changing client base in order to better represent those clients in the market. We need to recruit and develop leaders from 100 percent of the population. Warren Buffett once said, "We've seen what 50 percent of our human capacity can accomplish. Visualize what 100 percent can do." He gets it.

In 2012, the then current executive team was developing our second wave growth plan, which demanded not only high innovation and creativity, but also healthy debate. It was then that Kevin Maggiacomo and Mark Van Ness recognized that growing a company with an all-white male executive team and statutory board and having an Advisor base dominated by white male baby boomers presented three significant challenges for growth.

First, the all-male management team featured zero diversity, no balanced perspective and, quite frankly, a lower collective group IQ for a company intent on sustainable growth. Individual concerns were being set aside for fear of upsetting the group's balance—essentially a *don't criticize my ideas and I won't challenge yours* dynamic. Groupthink was firmly entrenched and we weren't generating good ideas.

The second issue was that historically at SVN there had been a disproportionate number of women who were high performers when compared to the actual number of women in the company at that time. However, when the company was restructured in 2009, there hadn't been any intentionality to recruiting and developing talent from Buffett's 100 percent of the population.

And third, while the lack of gender balance is an issue affecting all companies and industries, it seems especially deep-rooted in commercial real estate brokerage. Women and people of color simply aren't playing a big enough role in brokerage, and this is to the detriment of the industry as a whole and companies in particular.

Even if you did not care about the morality and social imperative of it all, hiring the best talent from the most diverse pool is a bottom line issue. Even the most cursory of Google searches will identify a multitude of studies showing that companies that purposely include women in the rank and file, executive suites and board rooms enjoy stronger financial performance and higher creativity and innovation. So, tackling this problem at SVN was both an issue of doing the right thing and of driving deal flow to increase firm productivity.

On the production side, for Kevin Maggiacomo and the rest of the leadership team, achieving gender balance within the SVN Advisor base to more accurately reflect the changing demographics was an obvious, no-brainer business move. Women are outnumbering men in terms of new undergraduate and graduate degrees, more women than ever before are entering the asset and property management business, and the brokerage clients of tomorrow will reflect these trends.

Kevin Maggiacomo described the evolution of SVN's commitment to diversity as follows:

"Back in 2013, it was obvious we were paying a steep price for our lack of diversity. And it was a bit of a punch in the gut to realize I had been growing SVN's business oblivious to an unconscious—and dangerous—bias that was holding both the company and me back. That same year I had the honor of delivering a TEDx talk on diversity and what followed was a transition from diversity and gender equality as an interest to a passion. I soon recognized that bigger results would follow once I put a program in place that shifted our leadership balance.

"But I also knew it was going to take a steep commitment to change viewpoints. Changing hearts and minds doesn't happen by simply evangelizing. Plus, biases and traditions don't happen by accident; they are designed—consciously or otherwise—to keep a certain group in power. And those who run the show seldom champion change. So commercial real estate has institutional barriers to entry for anyone who is a woman or minority. It's a traditionally white, male industry so for generations recruiting into commercial real estate has been focused on closed homogenous networks.

"Sure, there will be the occasional company with

superstar women in high-level positions, but they are the exception that proves the commercial real estate glass ceiling rule. Ask most young women about their best career options and commercial real estate would barely be a blip on their professional radar. Even in firms that are receptive to women, the same glass ceiling issues we hear about in other male-dominated industries affect the number making it through to the senior levels. No wonder commercial real estate is not appealing to young women considering their future careers.

"While the problem is widespread it is not insurmountable. But we need to be proactive and men need to step up to the plate. Senior executives—both male and female—need to think outside the usual box and look beyond the expected, traditional candidates when hiring or promoting. They need to focus on skills, results, and the benefits of diversifying their leadership team. It's tackling things as basic as: *"does our advertising material feature all men?"* to more complicated aspects like how do we eliminate any glass ceilings and subtle biases against the women and people of color we do have so that they can succeed at SVN.

"The reality is that men hold the preponderance of commercial real estate leadership positions, so if we're to see meaningful change across the industry men need to take action. Gender initiatives have traditionally focused on improving women's participation in the workplace, but it's not a women's issue, it's actually a human issue and there has to be a shift towards making gender a gender-neutral problem and opportunity. What is required here is a completely restructured view of what commercial real estate leadership should look like.

"With that in mind, a year and half following my TEDx talk, the SVNIC executive and leadership team had become balanced at 50 percent, and we restructured SVN's executive team, which at times has actually been imbalanced with 60 percent women but is hitting on all cylinders. In total, we operate as a think tank for new ideas, we aren't striving for harmony in our meetings, our profitability has increased by more than 100 percent, our risk is at an all-time low and we're trending positive across all key performance indicators."

A View from the Other Side [Why it's Tough to be an Only]

In 2012, Kevin Maggiacomo hired me to serve as the company's first chief platform officer, where I was responsible for more fully building out the company's platform of tools, training and resources. In 2014, I was promoted to Chief Operating Officer and became one of the few women in the c-suite in a national or international commercial real estate firm.

What's it like to be a woman in the commercial real estate industry today? It's probably very similar to being a woman in venture capital, technology, or science. You are often the only woman in the room, and that can be isolating. It can also be a great advantage. In my early years in commercial real estate almost everyone remembered me because I stood out. But it was clear that in certain situations my gender made some people uncomfortable, and then there were those who felt strongly that women did not even belong in the room. Fortunately, I grew up competing with and against the boys in sports so being the only female in the room and having to prove my right to be there was pretty much standard fare for me. This is why SVN has been such a remarkable place to work. While the industry might still have biases, the amount of productivity that happens at SVN offices due to the lack of bias is unparalleled.

I do believe that Kevin's commitment to gender balance goes beyond recruiting and has added value to leadership decisions at SVN. Having gender balance in a company setting allows you to break through unintentional barriers to progress. For example, look at your company's marketing collateral; if there is no gender or ethnic diversity represented, some of the best candidates, and even clients, will infer that your company does not want to work with them. And that is something your management team might not pick up on if they all look like the people in your marketing collateral.

Diversity also helps with creative problem-solving. When you bring people with different experiences to sit at the table and debate issues, you have a better chance at finding the best solutions. With diversity on the management team, you are less likely to have a company run by yes-men, or in the cases where the leadership is all women, yes-women.

A lot has been written about why women lack equality in the workplace. Everyone has a theory: there's a confidence gap; women don't ask—or when they do, they get penalized; they don't apply for positions unless they are fully qualified; and we even have studies that show women are lied to more than men in negotiations. These are all part of the same problem. If you pare it down, the underlying factor is that women rarely get the benefit of the doubt in a business situation.

Today's leaders need to change their frame of reference on how they judge performance. Eliminate gender-based doubts and focus on results, skills, and raw talent when deciding who should tackle that tough assignment or get that promotion. In other words, don't create performance obstacles that only exist in your own perception. Outdated stereotypes are a huge detriment to everybody in the workplace. If she's as qualified as the next guy, then give her the same benefit of the doubt as you would him.

Right now, the brokerage and investment areas of commercial real estate are only about 20 percent female; and the percentage gets much lower the further up the ladder one goes. While there are more women in property management, this means that any change is going to be slow. It will take a deliberate change in recruiting to make a difference in the industry.

However, once we get more diversity in the pipeline, sales is a results-oriented business, so it should eliminate the biases. My prediction is that the industry will be slow to change in the next five years, but if we put intentionality into our recruiting efforts, SVN offices can be leaders for change. In fact, we have a built-in advantage. The SVN shared fee, plus our open and transparent approach to marketing properties, creates a structured, common sense environment for Advisors and clients. Women, people of color, and other brokers new to the industry simply want to know the rules of the game. They don't want to change the rules. Nor do they want special treatment. They just want to make sure the game is not rigged against them. The more we get our SVN Difference message out to the world, the more we will be able to recruit talented women and men as both Advisors and clients.

Chapter Eight

Marketing Properties the SVN® Way

Chapter Author: Solomon Poretsky

Solomon Poretsky is our chief development officer. In this chapter, he outlines the math behind the SVN Difference when it comes to listing and marketing properties the SVN® way.

From our founding, the SVN brand has been focused on maximizing value for our clients through the practice of compensated cooperation. We believe that clients get better results when we: 1.) Expose property listings to the entire universe of brokers and their clients; and 2.) compensate those brokers with half of the total fee. And we know that we should do this on every transaction.

This idea just makes sense. After all, it is a basic economic tenet that as demand increases, prices follow. This rule holds true in the consumer market, in financial markets, and in the residential real estate market. While this concept has always been a part of the SVN value proposition, we have been on a mission to prove that this rule is true in the commercial real estate world. In 2016, we surveyed 15,000 transactions spanning ten states over 10 years, and conclusively proved that cooperation works. All other factors being equal, properties that sold through broker cooperation achieved prices that were, on average, 9.6% higher on a price-per-square-foot basis.

Understanding Cooperation

In a cooperative transaction, different brokers represent the seller and buyer, or the landlord and tenant. This happens when the broker representing the listing side promotes the property publicly to other brokers from outside of his or her practice. Giving an asset broad exposure increases the total number of potential buyers or tenants who would consider it, see it, and write offers or Letters of Intent on it. More offers bring more competition, which ultimately improves the price, the terms of the transaction, or both.

Even so, many brokers will claim that cooperation is unnecessary or undesirable. And their arguments appear to effectively convince clients into letting them represent properties without cooperating - especially when it comes to sales. This continues to happen, even though cooperative transactions are the norm in the residential world. To understand the disparity, take a look at the numbers: Of the 14,793 commercial sale transactions that we surveyed, just one out of six were cooperative. The remaining 12,335 deals were transacted by a single brokerage firm. Applying the 9.6%

formula of missing value means that clients may have collectively missed out on $7.2 billion in sale price.

It's worth noting that most states realize that broker cooperation is in the client's best interest. This is why many have laws requiring brokers to make a special disclosure when they are serving as a dual agent and representing both sides of the transaction - even in commercial transactions, which can be subject to less stringent regulations. Some states even ban dual agency due to the potential for a conflict of interest.

The Survey and Data Set

To assess the effect of cooperation, we obtained 15,440 sale transaction records from Real Capital Analytics (RCA), a well-respected third-party commercial real estate research firm. After removing records with incomplete information, 14,793 remained. These spanned ten states in the Western, Southwestern, Midwestern, and Eastern regions of the U.S., and covered sales with prices between the RCA minimum of $2.5 million up to an upper limit of $20 million.

The data set included transactions from the four major asset classes - apartment, industrial, office, and retail buildings. In addition, the data set spanned the period from 2006 through 2015, covering a broad range of market types - strong, weak, and recovering.

It is important to note that the data included transactions from many different commercial real estate firms. Our report's conclusions apply to SVN, but also speak to cooperation's benefits across the entire commercial real estate industry.

Our Findings

Our findings were clear. Properties that sold through broker cooperation achieved an average selling price per square foot of $108.37. Those that sold with the involvement of only a single brokerage achieved an average selling price per square foot of $98.84. In other words, broker cooperation generated a sale price that was 9.6% higher than single-brokerage firm transactions.

As a part of our analysis, we tested the data to find out if there was any bias. First, we compared the sizes of the two pools of assets. The average property sold with broker cooperation was 57,142 square feet, while properties sold by single firms averaged 59,651 square feet. This 4.2% difference was too small to significantly impact the price of the two pools of properties.

In addition, we looked at the data to see if the positive impact of cooperation was tied to a certain property type. While the impact of cooperation value ranged from a 6.1% price increase for office buildings to an 18.4% increase for apartments, the data was conclusive that every product type benefited from brokerage cooperation. Cooperation was also a net positive in every state tested.

Finally, to ensure that our data was not tainted by a small number of large transactions, we worked with an international team of economists, statisticians and consultants to conduct a regression analysis. That analysis, which used the natural logarithm of prices, showed a smaller increase in price - but still a very statistically meaningful one of 6.77%. Most importantly, this increase is greater than any increase in total fee that could be caused by cooperation.

Arguments Against Cooperation

Arguments against cooperation remain common in the greater commercial real estate brokerage community. Some brokers say that the buying pool for an asset is so finite that there is no need to expose the asset more broadly. Others claim that even if the buying pool is large, their databases are so large that they span the entire universe of potential buyers. Still others claim that broad marketing could harm the operations of the property, and either reduce its net operating income and ultimate value, or even render it unmarketable.

All three arguments are misleading. Let me tell you why.

First, it is theoretically true that a poorly designed marketing campaign can carry the risk of harming the operations of certain types of commercial real estate. Properties like hotels, senior living facilities, and others that have large employee bases, could lose workers if information about the sale leaks to the wrong people at the wrong time and/or in the wrong context. However, this concern rarely applies to properties in core asset types. In addition, if broad marketing exposure was harmful to properties, those that received this exposure would sell for lower prices than those that brokers kept close to their proverbial vests.

Second, it is impossible for any one broker to be able to predict the entire buyer universe or to have that universe in his or her (or his or her firm's) database. The buying pool is too large and too fluid. Cross-border transactions typically account for approximately two-thirds of the market's velocity. While it is theoretically possible that a broker in Kansas City, Missouri could know all the likely buyers in Kansas City, Kansas, it is extremely unlikely that the broker could know every potential buyer in Seattle, Miami, or Boston.

Knowing the likely buyers isn't enough anymore. As institutional investors and high net-worth private investors continue increasing their allocations to real estate, more and more new capital provided by new buyers is entering the market. These non-traditional buyers - many of whom have different investment criteria than other real estate buyers - are frequently not represented by traditional commercial real estate firms, making it impossible to reach them without an extremely broad campaign, fueled by the power of compensated cooperation.

Cooperation, Client Value, and SVN

The data from the market is clear: Cooperation works. While our research shows that it delivers an additional 9.6% per square foot in sale price, the actual impact on a seller's net proceeds is even greater when one considers that many transactions include fixed costs like loan pay-offs. On an $8 million sale that includes the retirement of a $4 million loan and 6.5% costs of sale, the 9.6% increase in sale price generates almost 21% more in net proceeds for the seller.

The benefits of broker cooperation exist regardless of who does it. Any firm that creates a truly robust market for an asset can generate higher selling prices for their clients. However, only one commercial real estate brand has cooperation built into its platform, its training, and its ethos - SVN. With our commitment to share 50% of the fee 100% of the time, we leverage the benefit of cooperation for every client. This is an important story to tell - and a crucial differentiator in the market.

Conclusion: SVN's Why

In the traditional model, where brokerage firms require buy-side brokers to procure their fees from the buyer, costs are not reduced for sellers, and brokers are discouraged from working on the deal.

Potential investors are everywhere—yet they often have established relationships with real estate agents or advisors. These investors, especially the more exclusive ones, are unlikely to respond to cold calls and traditional marketing. The most direct access to these individuals is to share information and provide incentivized compensation to their existing trusted advisors.

The days of hoarding information are over. It's inefficient and limits the demand for an asset. Social media and real-time connectivity tools allow advisors to reach a greater number of brokers and potential buyers in an efficient and more cost-effective manner than ever before. But it's not enough to just market the property in real time; an advisor needs a consistent, transparent co-brokerage incentive attached to each asset to truly drive demand and a higher price.

Author and marketing consultant Simon O. Sinek says people don't buy *what* you do; they buy *why* you do it. SVN was founded on the tenets of fee sharing, collaboration, and on an unwavering commitment to putting the clients' interests first. This SVN point of differentiation inspires action. It causes sellers to want to list with our advisors. It causes advisors to want to join the SVN organization. But it's not just a tenet. Research has shown that when listings are open to the widest audience, and when there are proper incentives in place, properties are sold for a higher price.

The bottom line is that compensated cooperation—the SVN Difference—is maximizing results for clients. We do this because it's right, and because it's our why.

Chapter Nine

The Power of a Franchise System

For all the things that differentiate the SVN® brand, perhaps our biggest differentiator is that we are a franchise operation. There was a time in the commercial real estate industry when franchising was the F-word, never to be used. Yet our franchise owners have come to realize that this is the best way to provide global, firm-level service with true local decision-making and entrepreneurialism.

Franchising done well can empower small, medium and large independent and entrepreneurial business enterprises across a variety of market sizes and locations. While it presents unique challenges from our end at SVNIC as a franchisor, all our offices have the ability to operate and execute transactions at a national level and it doesn't matter if they are in a gateway, secondary or even tertiary market. We provide the tools, resources and training so our 200+ franchise offices can focus on building their business.

I believe the franchise business model and the dedication to collaboration is the best opportunity for our company to lead the way in diversifying the ownership and advisor base but also maximizing our brand's potential for sustainable growth. This is where we come full circle. We are dedicated to inclusion, —whether it be through gender balance, diversity, new talent from outside the industry regardless of age or background —and to providing everyone with opportunities that they otherwise would not have. The SVN platform just makes more sense for anyone—male or female, regardless of background or ethnicity. We are also an ideal place for anyone destined to hit the commercial real estate ceiling at one of the large national firms or the self-starter who wants to own their own business and grow it their way.

We are a commercial real estate franchise with over 200 offices, giving us more locations in the U.S. than any other commercial real estate firm. We have more locations because our platform works in secondary and tertiary markets, and in gateway cities. In the spirit of full disclosure, the truth is we don't have as many resources as our billion-dollar competitors, but our franchisees keep the majority of their profits and reinvest in their own businesses. SVN is home to entrepreneurial independents working together under a single brand. And our model supports the fact that we can have offices in secondary and tertiary markets—a play that doesn't make sense for the larger firms.

The franchise model also supports our overall mission of being a more inclusive company. Traditionally, women and people of color have had success in franchising. We encourage every real estate professional to consider joining or owning an SVN franchise because it gives them an enhanced platform while keeping the characteristics that make their companies and businesses unique.

SVN didn't come out of the gate in 1987 as a national franchise company. SVN was launched as a regional firm specializing in investment sales. By 1990, SVN had ten offices and became the first commercial brokerage to connect all agents and offices. Then, a decade later we tested the water by creating licensing arrangements with individuals working in other states. Eventually, we transitioned these licenses into full franchises.

We experienced significant growth as we added more franchises. In 2008, we transitioned to a franchise-only model as part of a company restructuring after deciding to focus on the side of our business that was progressive, innovative, and revolutionary. We elected to exit the corporate store brokerage business, sold our corporate offices in August of that year, and became a pure franchisor. We began to automate and outsource major components of every one of our cost centers. This brought scalability and variability to our operating expense model, and it allowed us to reduce costs while redeploying those savings into investments in profitability tools for our Advisors.

The timing of becoming a full franchise company in 2008 was fortuitous. There are no doubts that this strategic move enabled SVN to navigate the Great Recession. No one could have honestly predicted the 90% decline in sales volume and the 40% decline in pricing that occurred one and two years respectively after the initiative started

Our SVN franchise model aligns with both the move towards lean and agile companies where brokers can work effectively inside and outside the main office and it gives Advisors the freedom to be entrepreneurial. In addition, Advisors have access to leading edge marketing, training, business, and technology systems; more opportunities for a diverse set of commercial real estate professionals to own their own business; and inclusion in a diverse community of experts around the country.

An important aspect of franchising is that SVN Advisors and their clients benefit from being a local company invested in their community, while also enjoying access to leading edge, top-line national resources. What we have today is a sustainable business model with an infrastructure that provides technology and profitability tools and in which all stakeholders benefit.

What Makes for a Successful Franchisee?

We have just spent an entire book on the SVN culture, so it should not be a surprise that the number one factor we look for in a franchisee, their brokers and operating staff, is cultural fit. Our system works for those who understand the SVN Difference and who bring their own unique talents and professional acumen. We are inclusive, not uniform. Every market, every client, every office is independently operated while representative of the overarching SVN brand.

According to George Slusser, our Chief Growth Officer and the leadership team member responsible for bringing in new franchisees, strong SVN offices are culturally compatible, entrepreneurially-minded, and growth-oriented.

"The primary trait that we seek in a partner and team member is cultural compatibility. A successful SVN office must be willing to help reshape the commercial real estate industry by adhering to our core covenants. This includes always putting the client first by sharing fees and information with the entire brokerage community. It means providing comprehensive services to clients by pulling in the right team members from across our SVN ecosystem for both experience and execution. It requires a dedication not just to the SVN brand and all it stands for, but also to our families and our communities.

"An ideal office is also very entrepreneurial-oriented, with a strong desire to control their future through local ownership of a competitive real estate services company. They will have an individual at the helm who has demonstrated throughout their career strong leadership skills, professional competency, and the ability to create a collaborative culture.

"Successful SVN franchisees will have a vision for growing a quality firm focused on adding ethical and highly trained advisors. Our SVN headquarters team will assist with the plan and the implementation but the franchisee must have the passion for achieving the goals. The growth objective is not necessarily to be the largest but to be recognized as providing the absolute best service to clients and their market."

If our franchisees and their Advisors use tools we provide and embrace the SVN core covenants to guide everything they do with and for the SVN brand, they set themselves up for success—if they are willing to work hard. None of our tools or covenants will matter if you don't work hard and if you don't think and act like a champion. You can master the art and science of commercial real estate brokerage, but if hard work and grit don't undergird that, then none of that will matter.

Grit is passion and perseverance for long-term goals. Grit is having stamina. Grit is sticking with your future, day in, day out, not just for the week, not just for the month, but for years, and working really hard to make that future a reality. Grit is living life like it's a marathon, not a sprint. We're looking not for a flash in the pan year, but for sustainable success. For anyone striving to succeed the secret is not genius or even talent but a special blend of passion and persistence. Our franchise model helps those with that passion, persistence, and grit succeed. We tell our franchisees: *You have the SVN systems for success, get focused, and use them moving forward. Be disciplined, be in it to win it, set your goals high, and don't stop until you get there.*

Chapter Ten

SVN® Going Forward

That's the story of how SVN got to where it is today as a company and as a brand with a purpose. What happens next? This is how CEO and president, Kevin Maggiacomo put it when he gave his company address in February 2017.

"I want to close with a look at our goals moving forward. It remains unclear how today's macroeconomic conditions will impact commercial real estate markets. What is clear is that our industry will be impacted. Globalization, technology and demographic shifts are changing the way we live and work, and commercial real estate will always play a defining role, whether it is on the smaller investment end or larger institutional product.

"But regardless of the market forces, success and growth do not happen by accident; they take planning. So

SVN has developed a long-term strategic plan that is goal-oriented and informed by big risks and bold thinking while maintaining our culture, our commitment to shared value, and the SVN Difference.

"Our goal is to grow to $1 billion in SVN system revenue between now and 2027 and $500 million in the next 60 months by leveraging growth capital that will be invested in three key areas, each designed to increase deal flow throughout the organization. One such area is domestic expansion. There are more than 380 metropolitan statistical areas in the U.S. and gaining SVN coverage in every one will expand our platform so that we can create more opportunities for entrepreneurs who want to be franchisees, brokers and new to the business candidates who want to be SVN advisors, and the broader community of owners, investors and tenants who will benefit from having access to the unique SVN platform and all that it does to drive amazing benefits for them.

"Another is to expand the SVN brand internationally so that the sun never sets upon it. Since 2015, we've launched offices in Canada, Mexico, South Korea, Romania, Russia and Australia. Our goal is to build out the globe in a synergistic manner, wherein the benefits of a borderless market are delivered to all our stakeholders.

"But the biggest part of our growth will be from our franchisees collectively growing their businesses. To that end we have invested considerably in Advisor and managing director training programs designed to be a major strategic mechanism for our growth. The SVN System for Growth™ is an intensive Advisor training program aimed at increasing brokerage productivity, while the SVN | Elite Program is a multi-platform, year-long curriculum where the best and brightest SVN managing directors learn from each other.

"I'll try not to be too cliché here, but paramount to success in today's economy is for all of us to get outside our comfort zones. There will not be a return to old days and old ways of commercial real estate. Without being overly simplistic, I believe that those who are more agile and more adaptive are best equipped for success in the long-term. Those who change their approaches to reflect new and changing markets; who adopt new tools and resources; who empower talent and diversity of thought will be the ones who thrive. Those who do not might fall by the wayside. The old ways in which properties were acquired and financed, brokered and appraised, are gone, and they are not coming back. The need to change, to be creative, develop new verticals and partnerships is imperative.

"Fortunately, at SVN, we embrace difference. We are different, and we are successful. We are successful in part because we are different.

"You've heard me say before that SVN is not just a brand or a traditional business, but a purpose-driven business - and it's our commitment to create economic value from our core values. When we say that we're built to create amazing value with our clients, colleagues and our communities, what we're saying is that our success comes from the success of everyone we touch. It comes from creating opportunity for a diverse pool of applicants, encouraging more people to experience the life-changing opportunities of a career in commercial real estate than at any other firm. Bringing intentionality to recruiting, training and developing under-represented advisors is a clear shared value growth strategy implemented not to be philanthropic, but because it is strategically intelligent and aligns with our higher ambitions.

"Using the power of our real estate businesses to improve the communities in which we live – by focusing on solving societal problems - is also strategically intelligent. At SVN, our decision-makers live and work in their communities. Many of you have steered your practices towards community revitalization, bringing in developers and tenants who repurpose tired assets and create jobs in your communities - and these have been solid additions to your bottom lines. Our creation of a shared value network with the entire commercial real estate industry is not just good business; it's smart business.

So, $1 billion, one decade, one culture. That's where our brand with a purpose is going. Diversity, shared value, and the SVN Difference is how we will get there ... together."

* * *

With those words by Kevin Maggiacomo, we kick off our next phase of growth. We will continue to add offices in key markets and support our existing offices as they grow into full-service enterprises. But I want to close this book with another perspective. In 2017, after several of our offices around the globe had been threatened by natural disasters including hurricanes, floods, fires and earthquakes, it started to feel really personal. These offices, their managing directors, Advisors and staff are all part of the SVN family. That's when it dawned on me that in my 25-year plus career, I have never before described a company as my family. However, that's part of the SVN Difference. We may be in more than 200 separate locations, but we are still all on the same team and part of the same family. And, I, for one, am especially grateful to be a member and look forward to the future of the SVN brand.

About the Author

Diane Danielson is the Chief Operating Officer of SVN International Corp., one of the largest commercial real estate franchises in the U.S. with 200+ offices in six countries. As COO, Danielson oversees operations and spearheads strategic growth and development initiatives. She is a former attorney and an accomplished speaker with over 25 years of experience in the commercial real estate and technology industries. She is a graduate of Colgate University, and Boston College Law School.

Made in the USA
Monee, IL
10 August 2021